You Might Be a Golf Nut If...

You Might Be a Golf Nut If . . .

Randy Voorhees

STARK BOOKS

an Andrews McMeel
Publishing Imprint

00 01 02 03 04 BIN 10 9 8 7 6 5 4 3 2 1

Voorhees, Randy.
  You might be a golf nut if— / Randy Voorhees.
      p. cm
  ISBN 0-7407-1154-7 (pbk.)
    1. Golf—Humor. I. Title

PN6231.G68 V66 2000
796.352—dc21   00-41004

Book design by Holly Camerlinck

For Sarah and Carol

Acknowledgments

I would like to thank Mark Gola, John Monteleone, Stacia Nero, Mike Corcoran, Jeff Neuman, Rob Taylor, Tom Ferrell, Allan Stark, and Joan Mohan for their contributions to this book. (In fact, I doubly thank Allan Stark, my editor at Andrews McMeel, since he agreed to publish the book.) Special thanks to all you Golf Nuts out there for wearing your hearts on your sleeve.

Introduction

What is a Golf Nut?

I define a Golf Nut as a person whose intense love for the game has destroyed all balance in their life. They have irreparably damaged their personal and business relationships, because their very being is consumed by the singular pursuit of putting a little white ball into a hole four and one-quarter inches in diameter. Nothing else matters—not you, not me, not health or hygiene. A Golf Nut is the type of person who would bet his only daughter in a skins game. To paraphrase a song refrain, "They've come undone."

Sure, most all of us who play golf are at some point overcome by the challenges, frustrations, and rewards of the game. We even show some symptoms that characterize a Golf Nut: we putt balls in the office, we chip in the backyard, we consider

Myrtle Beach a fine place to vacation, and we dress in clothing best described as "unfortunate." But most of us realize that we're never going to replicate Jack Nicklaus's swing or play a round at Pine Valley, and besides, we have jobs and families that demand and deserve our attention. A Golf Nut makes no such concessions. If we are curmudgeonly about life outside of golf, Golf Nuts are misanthropic; they always take it one step further.

A Golf Nut receives birthday and holiday cards from the mayor of Myrtle Beach. A Golf Nut wouldn't dress in a plain pattern or color if you held a gun to his head, and the spouse of a Golf Nut understands that if she wants to spend quality time with the one she loves, she had better learn how to caddie or hit a two-iron off a hanging lie.

Golf Nuts are everywhere. In Minnesota, the "Land of Ten Thousand Lakes," Golf Nuts are willing to hit their ball, then row to it. They go to Las Vegas *for the golf.* In New York, a Golf Nut wouldn't hesitate to confront a Mafia boss over a questionable free drop. Golf Nuts are nearly as plentiful in America as lawyers. They're like divorcées: everybody knows one.

For purposes of this book, the term "Golf Nut" is one of derision. But Golf Nuts don't see it that way; they interpret the label as a badge of honor. It isn't important whether you use this book to find fodder for poking fun at a Golf Nut near you, or you take pride in pointing to an entry and saying, "Yup, that's me." What is important is that you take these jibes in good spirit. After all, golf is supposed to be fun, right?

You Might Be a Golf Nut If . . .

You closely monitor the
price fluctuations of titanium futures.

You installed a custom seat belt in your car
to hold your golf bag.

Your car has a bumper sticker that says
"Thank you for going spikeless."

You own more than three articles
of go-to-hell, lime-green clothing.

The mayor of Myrtle Beach sends you
a birthday card every year.

You believe you really *are* Tiger Woods.

You have the word "dormie"
tattooed on your arm.

There are little golden bears
imprinted on your underwear.

You married your wife because
her brother is a scratch golfer
and you needed a ringer for the
member-guest tournament.

You celebrate Cinco de Mayo
by masquerading as Lee Trevino.

When playing miniature golf,
you meticulously survey each putt.

You rake leaves using a Vardon grip.

You won't watch baseball
because the action is too fast.

You know the swingweight and
kickpoint of your Weed Eater.

Nevada Bob's holds a lien on your home.

You make a few practice strokes
before you sign your name.

You drink and smoke because, hey,
John Daly still hits it long.

You once wrote a poem about divots.

As a hobby, you collect
antique sprinkler heads.

For light reading, you keep a copy
of the *Official Rules of Golf*
on the nightstand.

You relish the thought of turning fifty
so you can play the forward tees.

You can say "You're still away"
in nineteen languages.

Despite being fired eight times,
you steadfastly refuse to let your boss win.

You've ever programmed the VCR
to tape the latest golf infomercials.

You think ankle socks are masculine.

You've ever hired a caddie to make love
to your wife so you could spend more time
at the twenty-four-hour driving range.

Your neighbors place
protective netting over their homes.

The Golf Channel televises your garage sales.

You insure your driver for more than your car.

You decided where to live
based on how easy it is to get
a tee time there.

Your handicap is lower than
your doctor's because you spend
less time at the office than he does.

Your first woodshop project was a Stimpmeter.

The IRS allowed you to declare
your home course starter as a dependent
on your tax return.

You spend more money on
sweater vests than you do on food.

You store your putter in a safe-deposit box.

You can tell the difference between a balata ball and a two-piece ball . . . blindfolded.

Your mail-order bride is from Scotland . . . and her name is Angus.

You think that the cemetery
is a great place to work on
your short game.

You own more than one
logoed umbrella.

You have the pro shop on speed dial.

Your burial plot is a pot bunker
that was designed by Pete Dye.

You whittle your own
mahogany tees.

You believe national parks
are a waste of prime golf real estate.

You wear your lower-back pain
as a badge of honor.

Your clubs fly first-class
and your spouse flies coach.

You took your family to Disney World
for the golf courses.

You know what the terms "slope"
and "equitable stroke control" mean
and you're able to work them
into your everyday conversation.

Your license plate says
"SNAPHOOK1."

You own a dog named Hosel.

You think that anyone
who protects wetlands is a Communist.

Your golf shoes double as your dress shoes.
(That's the big advantage of
spikeless golf shoes.)

You borrowed money
from Nicky the Kneecapper
to buy JFK's clubs.

You "sshuussh" people during a golf telecast.

Your "wet" dreams
are about lateral hazards.

You turn yourself in
for minor traffic violations.

⊛ ⊛ ⊛

You've ever borrowed against your house
to settle a golf debt.

⊛ ⊛ ⊛

You have a yardage book
for your front lawn.

Your ball retriever has a pet name
. . . which you painted on the shaft.

You whisper golf metaphors to your wife
during lovemaking. *(Your smile is as inviting
as a mulligan off the first tee and your skin
is as soft as the cover of a new balata ball.)*

You believe that the person seated
furthest from the beer tap
should be served first.

Your champagne glasses are miniature replicas
of the Ryder Cup.

You've ever gotten into a shoving match
over the definition of "loose impediment."

You allow faster shoppers
to move ahead of you in the checkout line.

Your business card lists
your handicap and the slope rating
of your home course.

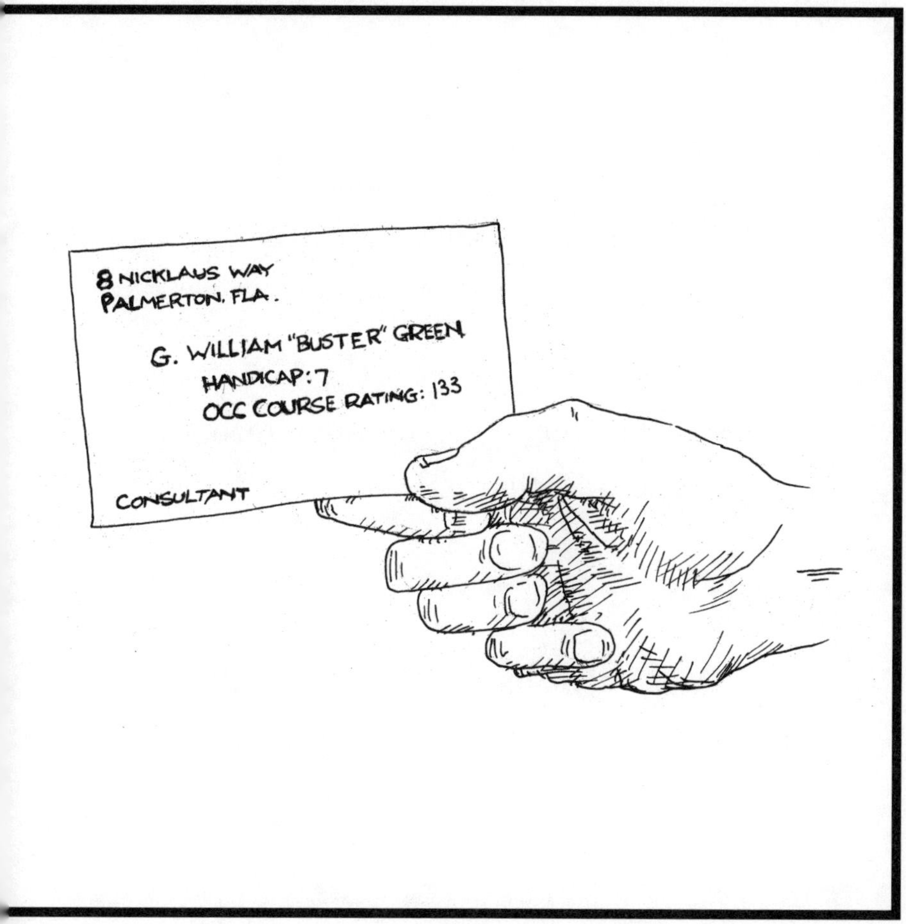
8 NICKLAUS WAY
PALMERTON, FLA.
G. WILLIAM "BUSTER" GREEN
HANDICAP: 7
OCC COURSE RATING: 133
CONSULTANT

Your hardwood floor is
tongue and square grooves.

You buy bug spray and sunscreen
by the case directly from the manufacturer.

You're available to take phone calls
only during lightning storms or frost delays.

You once spray-painted Arnold Palmer's name
on a highway overpass.

You maintain a supply of
colored golf balls for snowy days.

You're the only person on the nude beach
with a sand wedge in his hand.

You have a ball washer
in your laundry room.

Directions to your house include
"a driver and wedge from the
putting green."

You pledge allegiance to the flagstick
. . . literally.

You named your daughter Bertha
and your son Ping.

You dye your hair blond
and paint your teeth white
to look like Greg Norman.

Your life's ambition is to play
the lead role in a movie about Jim Colbert.

You're most famous for being
"the man who stalked Nancy Lopez."

You wore a *visor* and gown
at your college graduation ceremony.

You've ever driven more than
a hundred miles to get a good deal
on plastic ball markers.

You think Judge Smales got a raw deal.

The perimeter of your secretary's
work space is marked by white stakes.

Scott Hoch makes the list of
the ten people you admire most.

You wept at the grave site of
Old Tom Morris.

The sandbox in the yard is not for the kids.

You own a framed painting of
the word "Shank" with a diagonal orange bar
through it.

🏌 🏌 🏌

You're the only man in the
neighborhood who grows gorse in his garden.

🏌 🏌 🏌

You refer to an extramarital affair
as "hitting a provisional."

Your children think all pencils
are three inches long.

You once asked Ben Crenshaw to
"be my valentine."

Your clubshafts were designed
by NASA engineers and are waterproof
down to six atmospheres.

There's a weather vane
on your cap.

You bought a llama
to save money on cart fees.

On the two days a year when you can't play,
you get your fix by pounding your head
against a brick wall for three hours
and chasing a greased pig for two.

You lost your only daughter in a skins game.

You quit your job, packed your clubs,
and moved three thousand miles
so that your zip code would not include
a digit higher than 4.

You truly believe you can
"Add Ten Yards to Your Drives"
by reading a golf magazine.

While showering, you hum
the CBS-Masters theme music.

You've ever tunneled your way
into a Masters tournament.

In an effort to learn Hogan's "secret,"
you drove head-on into a bus.

You refer to your wife as "the Old Triple-Bogey."

You bronzed your first pair of golf shoes.
(Bonus points if the shoes are sitting
on your mantelpiece.)

You keep a spare divot-repair tool and spike
wrench under the floor mat of your car.

You disciplined a child for touching your golf
trading cards collection.

Your dream job is president of
the Dottie Pepper fan club.

You've ever asked a greenkeeper for an autograph.

You haven't washed below the elbow since
shaking hands with Bobby Jones's second cousin.

You took a caddie to the prom.

You've ever dreamed about sharing
a deserted island with Fred Couples.

⊛ ⊛ ⊛

You've ever used the pickup line
"May I play through?"

⊛ ⊛ ⊛

You're famous for your Gene Littler imitation.

⊛ ⊛ ⊛

You've ever taken the time
to count the dimples on a Titleist.

At an intervention, Ben Crenshaw
and Tom Kite tell you that you're taking golf
"way too seriously."

Your Pebble Beach hat
is mentioned in your will.

To curry favor, you submit to five root canals
a year because your dentist is a member
at Pine Valley.

You are "posing" in the perfect
follow-through position in all
of your family photos.

You greet everyone by saying, "You da man!"

You honestly believe the
exploding-ball trick is cool.

You wear wraparound sunglasses
and copper bracelets to bed.

You can name the winners of the last five
Skins Games and how much they won.

It takes you and your playing
partners more than thirty minutes after a
round to compute and settle your wagers.

You use Quicken software to track
all of your golf expenses and revenues.

You have a separate walk-in closet
for your golf apparel.

You own a pair of golf sandals
and have proudly worn them
on the course.

You admire Fuzzy Zoeller's ability
to speak extemporaneously.

You thought Leslie Nielsen's book *Bad Golf
My Way* was funny.

Whenever you attend a sporting event,
you leave two tickets for Harry Vardon.

You know the names of
Jack Nicklaus's children and
where their birthmarks are located.

You know the maiden names of
every married woman ever elected
to the LPGA Hall of Fame.

You have your golf balls, tees, ball markers,
and bag personalized with your nickname,
"the Scrambler."

You built a one-sixteenth scale model of
the par-3 twelfth hole at Augusta National
for your Eagle Scout project.

You believe Gary McCord and Johnny Miller
are bona fide journalists.

You think Dan Jenkins is *still* funny.

Your best friends know your USGA
handicap index but not where you live.

You judge a day not just by your score, but
by how many extra tees and balls you find.

You carry the titanium Visa card.
(Yes, there really is such a thing.)

You've ever purchased clothes because they
looked good on Colin Montgomerie.

The only reason you work is
to restore some balance in your life.

You learned to write in Spanish
so you could be a pen pal to Sergio Garcia.

You can't sleep the night before
the telecast of the first round
of the Canon Greater Hartford Open.

You believe that country clubs are centers
of great cultural diversity.

Your spouse always begins
the dinner conversation by asking,
"What did you shoot today, honey?"

When you refer to the "King,"
you're talking about Arnie, not Elvis.

You think the beer cart and its buxom driver
are annoying distractions.

You've ever yelled at your mother
for picking up a six-inch putt
before you've conceded it.

You pass up happy hour with the guys
to get in a "late nine."

Your golf bag is armed with an alarm system.

You chastised your spouse for using an issue
of *Golf Digest* to kill a spider.

You often wax rhapsodic
about pronation and supination.

Your family can't remember the last time
they saw you without at least one glove
hanging from your back pocket.

There's a sign marking
your personal parking spot
at the driving range.

You hire David Leadbetter to entertain
at your five-year-old's birthday party.

All your jokes begin with,
"So this guy's standing on the first tee . . . "

You believe that "four is company,
five's a crowd."

You refuse to play any game in which
high score wins.

You can't wait for sports-marketing
behemoth IMG to go public
so you can "own a piece of Tiger Woods."

☉ ☉ ☉

You've undergone hypnosis as a means
of curing your slice.

☉ ☉ ☉

You pray for a drought
so that you'll get more roll on your drives.

You've ever slept on the first tee
so you could be first off in the morning.

Your spouse cited "an adulterous affair
with golf" as the reason for filing for divorce.

Your wife has ever referred to your Big Bertha
as the "other woman."

You've submitted to an exorcism as a means
of expelling the evil "yips" from your body.

When dining out with friends, you flip
a tee on the table to decide
who will pay the check.

After making love to your spouse,
you pull a tiny pencil from behind your ear
and jot down a number on a scorecard.

Your children can't play in the front yard
because you have the "cart paths only" rule
in effect.

When your children get noisy,
you raise both arms and hold aloft
a sign that reads "Quiet."

You've ever hired a baby-sitter
so you could go to the driving range.

You watched instructional videos
at your bachelor party.

You told your wife "not now" when
she went into labor during the final round
of the Masters.

You think Heaven looks a lot like Scotland.

You believe Ben Hogan was
an engaging conversationalist.

You can listen to a golf instructor
and understand *everything* he says.

You actually use your set of Three Stooges
Talking Head Covers.

You won't answer the phone because
Fred Couples doesn't. (He's "afraid someone
might be on the other end.")

You think JoAnne Carner would have made
a great Charlie's Angel.

You want to party with Ken Venturi.

The high school honor you're most proud of is being named "most likely to break 80."

You remember all three of Nick Faldo's wedding anniversaries but not your own.

You've ever asked a tour player for a lock of his hair.

You've spent more than one hour
of your life bouncing a ball off
the face of your wedge.

You stayed awake all the way through
the movie *Tin Cup*.

You've spent time on Dr. Bob Rotella's couch
. . . and you were awake.

You were once arrested for
stealing Arnold Palmer's trash.

You changed your name to Eldrick.

You'd rather swing like Steve Elkington
than like Austin Powers.

Your will states which set of clubs
you are to be buried with.

You forget that Augusta is also the name
of a city.

You park in handicapped spaces because, hell,
you're a 16.

Your sexual foreplay begins
with a waggle.

You applied for veteran's benefits
for time served in Arnie's Army.

The only dance floor your feet
ever touch is covered with grass.

While driving, you visualize golf holes
fitting into the land next to the road.

You are moved to tears every time you see
Tiger Woods hug his father.

You refer to the Pacific Ocean as
"the big water hazard adjacent
to Pebble Beach."

Before releasing your bowling ball,
you "read" the alley from
every conceivable angle.

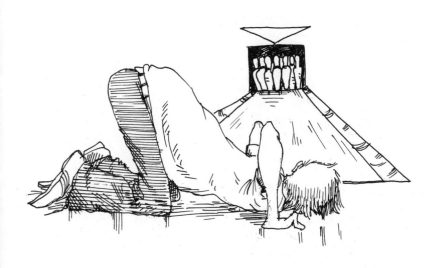

Your handicap is genuine.

❁ ❁ ❁

You think of life after forty
as "the back nine."

❁ ❁ ❁

You've skulled 1,412 consecutive
wedge shots trying to duplicate the one
you backed up.

Your left hand is whiter than milk.

Federal Express delivers all your packages
"in care of the nineteenth hole."

The postman refers to your address
as "the golf house."

You've ever gone to a public beach
to practice fairway bunker shots.

You hang diplomas from golf
schools on your office walls.

You factor in barometric pressure
when making your club selection.

You swore off coffee because
caffeine is bad for short putting.

You once sued your boss for
welshing on a golf bet.

You refer to your mother-in-law
as "ground under repair."

You have a scrapbook that chronicles
your development as a golfer.
(Bonus points if you have pictures
of yourself as a baby golfer.)

You refer to the golf course as
your "special place."

Family members need an appointment
to visit you at the practice range.

You played thirty-six holes a day
during your honeymoon.

You would play with Gerald Ford
without wearing a helmet.

The beer-cart girl knows your life story,
including your SAT score, your wife's
maiden name, and the swing weight
of your irons.

You led the protest that convinced
your cable operator to offer the Golf Channel.

You've ever been the honoree at
the annual Gutta Percha Ball Festival.

You've become much better at
subtraction than addition.

You've ever bought a golf training aid
that you were too embarrassed
to show anyone.

You really believe that "with a little
more practice" you can make it on
the Senior Tour.

You believe that you could help Tom Watson
with his putting if he would only
return your phone calls.

You've ever called the network to report
a rules infraction you witnessed during
their broadcast.

You throw a club after hitting
a bad shot . . . on the computer.

You home-school your children
so they can spend more time working
on their swings.

You selected a college based on its proximity
to well-regarded public golf courses.

You look forward to rainy days
because it means the course will be
less crowded.

You don't even raise an eyebrow
when someone says, "Hey, check out
my ultralong, stiff shaft."

You stress out more about being late
for a tee time than being late for a wedding.

Your wife refers to your garage as
"the pro shop."

Five hundred dollars for a club
that promises five more yards
sounds like a pretty good deal.

You've ever uttered the statement, "I pured
a butterblade down the hairs, threw a dart
to the pad, and bossed the moss to win
the automatic at the last," and no one
in your family needed a translation.

You call in sick so you can change your grips.

The word "Bermuda" doesn't make you
think of an island.

You've ever referred to God as
an "outside agency."

You've ever referred to
unethical business practices as
"preferred lies."

You gave your putter a "time out"
for a week because it didn't listen to you
on the eighteenth green.

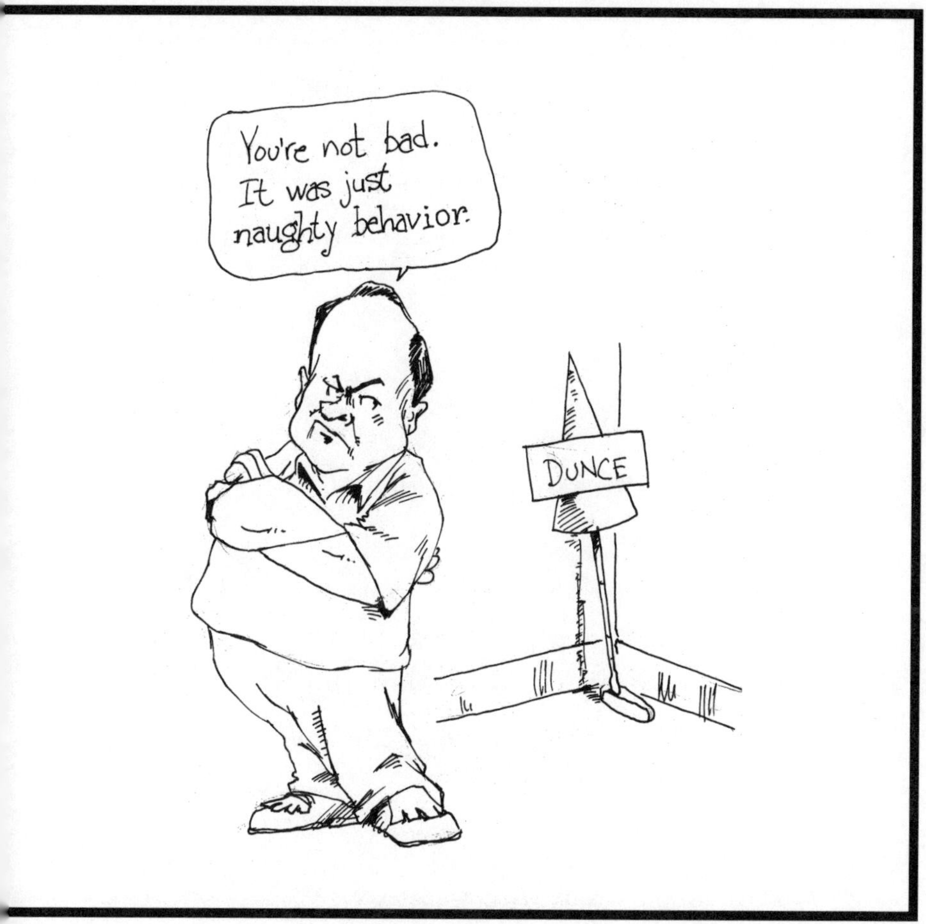
You're not bad. It was just naughty behavior.
DUNCE

You designed a Web page that provides
highlights of your most recent rounds.

Your E-mail address includes
the term "dogleg."

You can recall the details of the first par
you ever made . . . and you still have the ball.

You think the Gettysburg Address
is a different way of setting up to the ball.

You wish that golf was more expensive
so the courses wouldn't be so busy.

Your cap is equipped with a
battery-operated fan.

Your golf bag is so laden with material
that it's dangerous for anyone over thirty
to lift it.

You founded the local chapter of the
Singles Golf Association so you could meet
and date people who share your passion
for the game.

You dressed in knickers and tam-o'-shanter
or your driver's license photograph.

You really *enjoy* the challenge of playing
in the wind.

The new addition to your house is known as the "Golf Wing."

You find it entertaining to watch celebrities such as Joe Pesci, Jack Lemmon, or Clint Eastwood attempt to play golf.

When buying eggs, you check not for cracks but to see if they're out of round.

You think scoring a few lines means
doctoring your pitching wedge.

Cal Ripken publicly acknowledges
that *you* hold the record for
most consecutive days played.

You once confronted John Gotti about
taking an illegal drop.

You can distinguish one brand of club
from another by using only your sense of smell.

The "dollhouse" you built for your daughter
features a locker room, pro shop, and
indoor putting green.

While praying, you use the interlocking grip.

You view an electical storm as an opportunity to test the "even God can't hit a one-iron" theory.

You think about work
to get your mind off golf.

You invented a new language for use only
on the golf course and only by
"committed" players.

You recorded an entire year's worth of
good and bad bounces to determine
if the breaks truly do even out.

You carry a stopwatch so that you can time
the group ahead and document
their slow play.

You've played so much golf that you yawn
at the sight of a double-eagle.

You've never lost a club, because you don't
leave something that valuable on the ground
(and you count them after every shot).

You actually practice skipping balls
across bodies of water.

You can sense a shank before it happens.
(None of this "Where did that come from?"
with you.)

You redesigned your driveway
into a dogleg right configuration.

You've ever asked your parents to
"take the kids for a few days" so that you
and your spouse can work a few things out
. . . on the putting green.

Your young children think "quiet time" is the few seconds before Daddy makes his stroke.

You've ever committed a felony because you "needed money for greens fees."

You've ever traded sex for a new putter.

You've ever written a personal ad that began
with the words "Single, low-handicap,
male golfer seeks single, low-handicap,
female golfer."

The roof of your house is sodded
so as to simulate an elevated and
severely pitched green.

You really believe that science will find a cure
for the yips.

The members of your regular foursome are
paying for your anger-management program.

You know the year the first recorded shipment
of golf clubs and balls landed in America
from Scotland.

You seriously believe that the eagle
is America's national bird because
it represents excellence in golf.

You might slow your car for
a crossing cat or dog, but you
speed up at the sight of a
gopher or groundhog.

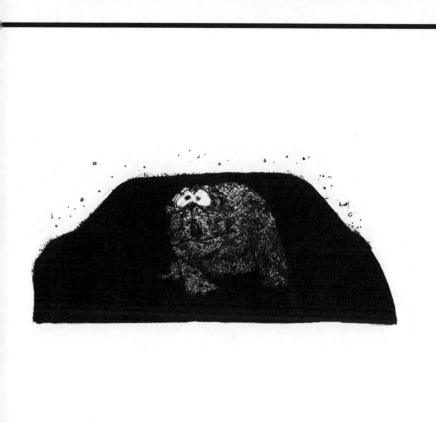

Your favorite limerick begins with
"I once played a course in Nantucket . . . "

❀ ❀ ❀

You've played all of *Golf Digest*'s
"Top 100 Courses in America" . . . this week.

❀ ❀ ❀

You winter in Scotland.

The highlight of your family reunion
was the chip-off between Uncle Trip
and Aunt Topsy.

You go to a mini-tour event in
North Dakota and don't need a program.

There's a life-sized cutout of
Tom Watson anywhere in your home.

Your sport-utility vehicle features
the Tiger Woods mud flaps.

You bought your parents his-and-her
lob wedges for their wedding anniversary
. . . and they don't play golf.

Another one hundred years of life
wouldn't provide enough days for you to wear
each of your logoed hats just once.

You divorced your first wife because
she wouldn't let you display your collection
of twenty-five hundred golf balls
in the living room.

You know exactly when the rule setting
the maximum allowable number of clubs
(fourteen) was established and why
that number was picked.

You use an old lob wedge
as a pooper-scooper.

You know that four-time U.S. Open
champion Mickey Wright is a woman.

You enjoy slow play because
there isn't anyplace else on earth
you'd rather be.

Your favorite CD is
The Best of Bagpipe Music.

You'd rather play golf with Juli Inkster
than wrestle with Xena the Warrior Princess.

Your wall safe contains any of the following:
scorecards of your five best rounds,
your hole-in-one ball, an autographed copy
of Gary Player's book *Bunker Play*, or a lock
of Jack Nicklaus's hair.

You have set up a trust fund
for your children's golf lessons.

You carry a picture of your putter
in your wallet.

You believe PGA Tour commissioner
Tim Finchem seems like a fun-loving guy
who would be comfortable drinking shots
and beers in a sports bar.

You go to Las Vegas for the golf.

You play in Florida . . . in the summer
. . . thirty-six holes a day.

You have a lifetime membership
at a miniature-golf course.

You hold the course record anywhere.

As long as they still sponsor the pro golf tours,
you'll never own anything other than
a Buick or Cadillac.

You really believe that your weekly visits
to the golf psychologist is
money well spent.

All your desk accessories feature a golf motif.

On report-card day, your kids know to enter
the house hollering "Fore!"

You once fired an employee
because he couldn't break 90.

Every pro shop within two hundred miles
of your home knows when you get a raise.

You award bonuses to your sales personnel
for reaching certain performance standards:
Birdie Level, Eagle Level, and
Double-Eagle Level.

You car windows and sunglasses are
tinted green.

You have a standing order for head covers
with the local seniors knitting club.

You move to a higher elevation
to add distance to your drives.

You hold the Guinness record
for most career shanks by an active golfer.

You steam-clean your head covers.

You often wear clothes so garish
they would make Cher blush.

You can't count past par.

You encouraged your children to quit school
and go to the driving range every day instead.

You actually believe you'll get better.

You actually believe that
perimeter-weighted irons are the greatest
invention in history . . . and metal woods
are a close second.

The most contentious part of your divorce
was over ownership of the
golf-club membership.

Your Christmas stocking is a shag bag.

Your new four-bathroom house boasts
cute little signs on the doors such as
"Hole No. 1."

You installed red stakes designating your
neighbor's yard as a lateral hazard.

You wear black and red on Sundays
because that is what Tiger does.

O.B. and S.O.B. are inexorably linked
in your postshot speech pattern—that is,
one automatically follows the other.

You pay to have Dave Pelz flown in
to work on your short-game problems.

You read the entire court transcript of the
trial between the PGA Tour and Casey Martin.

You're unhappy with a straight shot,
because you were trying to "work" the ball.

You've ever listened to golf on the radio.

You ever dragged a dead playing partner
for fourteen holes so that you could finish
your round before calling the coroner.

You blew off a child-custody hearing
to play in the club championship.

You've ever played a recovery shot
from the fast lane of a crowded interstate.

You've refused to declare
any ball unplayable, even one
lying next to an alligator.

They call you Lefty because you used
your right hand to retrieve a
golf ball lying next to an alligator.

They threw you out of the twelve-step
program at Golfers Anonymous, saying that
your addiction was "untreatable."

You've ever hit your best friend because
he coughed during your backswing.

You've ever climbed a barbed-wire fence
and eluded an angry dog to retrieve
a ninety-nine-cent golf ball.

You've ever screamed at a foursome of seniors,
"Hey, move your asses!"

You've ever asked that a debt
be repaid in golf balls.

You'd rather eat a live rat
than leave a birdie putt short.

⊛ ⊛ ⊛

You've ever asked your congressman
to look into the problem of slow play in golf.

⊛ ⊛ ⊛

All your towels are grass-stained.

⊛ ⊛ ⊛

The USGA has a file on you
that they've shared with the FBI.

You carry a tape measure in your golf bag
for settling those arguments about
"Who's away?"

You've ever written to "Dear Abby"
for advice on what to do about your
spouse's poor wedge play.

You buy every new book on negotiating
to help you get more strokes from your
match-play opponents.

You've ever attempted
to move a "loose impediment"
larger than your car.

Amen Corner tops your list
of most sacred places.

You really believe that talking
to a golf ball gets results.

You've left instructions that upon
your death your ashes are to be
scattered over the first fairway at the club.

You shave using soap and a one-iron.

Your single-digit handicap is
emblazoned on your forehead for
all to see (and envy).

You keep photographs of
Arnold Palmer's grandchildren
in your wallet.

You pick up your dates in a golf cart.

You experienced sympathy pains when
Jack Nicklaus had hip-replacement surgery.

You had soft spikes molded to the bottom
of your wedding-day dress shoes.

You were outraged when Mark McGwire's
record-tying home run received more
media coverage than Jeff Sluman's victory
over Steve Stricker in the Greater
Milwaukee Open.

You don't need a Stimpmeter to
tell at what speed your lawn is rolling.

You've played on two different
continents on the same day.

You once crossed the
international date line to extend
a golf vacation for another day.

You've ever flown the Concorde to catch
the final day of the Volvo German Masters.

You've ever declared a ball unplayable
in a lava flow.

You own a lead-lined sweater vest in case you're
forced to play through a nuclear winter.

You pace off the yardage on par-3s.

You know the molecular structures
of graphite and titanium.

You once hit into a foursome of Khmer Rouge
regulars who wouldn't invite you
to play through.

You lobbied Congress to put Harvey Penick
on a stamp.

You've ever rowed to your ball.

You enlisted in the army for the
reduced-rate greens fees.

You traded your grandmother's
engagement ring for a copy of Tiger Woods's
high school yearbook.

Your steering wheel was custom designed
by Golf Pride so you can practice your grip
while you drive.

You ask dinner guests to adjourn to the den
to view a videotape of your most recent session
at the "Swing's the Thing" golf school.

You send your golf gloves out for dry-cleaning.

You once burned a Union Jack
during Ryder Cup week.

You raised the topic of golf at a biker bar.

For you, Bermuda grass is an aphrodisiac.

You compile written scouting reports
on the other members of your club.

You became an organ donor
in exchange for a round at Augusta National.

You're on speed dial in the office
of every doctor who plays golf on Wednesday.

You have an established handicap
for computer golf games.

You've ever written an angry letter to the editor
about escalating greens fees.

You rub Viagra on your driver.

You commissioned Picasso to paint
a canvas of you standing over a putt.

You've ever torched a
woods or field to find your ball.

You practiced knockdown shots
during Hurricane Andrew.

You believe convicts would better serve society
by making wedges instead of license plates.

You once laid your body across a cart path to
protest the "cart paths only" rule.

You regret that you have but one
life to give for your country club.

You carry a lantern and candles in
your golf bag in case you run out of daylight
before completing fifty-four holes.

Your kids have a pull cart instead of
a little red wagon.

Your spouse demanded that you switch
to soft spikes after noticing the holes
in your bedsheets.

More than one tour player has a
restraining order against you.

You handed your USGA membership card
to a police officer, expecting him to
"give a break to a fellow golfer."

You once grounded one of your children
for not raking his sandbox after playing.

You read to your children from Harvey Penick's
Little Red Book.

Your insist that your wife refer to you as
"Iron Byron," because you think you are special
in bed and on the course.

You use old iron clubs to stake
your tomato plants.

You've ever practiced your swing
in your spouse's flower bed.

You've ever offered a pro golfer
money for a sample of his DNA.

More than one person has suggested
that you drink more and play golf less.

You retire to the "scorer's tent"
in your den to total up your bills.

You take your spouse out for an expensive
dinner to celebrate the anniversary
of the first time you played golf together.

You brag to single women
about your "clubhead speed."

You stamp all your balls
with your beeper number.

You scout the college ranks for golfers to add
to your fantasy golf team.

When the driving-range clerk sees you,
he asks, "The usual?"

You've ever called the post office to inquire
as to why your Golfsmith catalog
hasn't arrived yet.

You own a jigsaw puzzle of a bunker.

You own a stuffed likeness of your favorite
PGA Tour pro.

Your golf cart features four-wheel drive,
a CD changer, tinted glass, and does zero
to sixty in six seconds.

You use your scores to pick your lottery numbers.

You proposed to someone because you were
in love with their short game.

You tow your golf cart to vacation destinations.

You own a bumper sticker that reads
"C Flight Champion on Board."